Corkscrews
& Wine Antiques

A Collector's Guide

Corkscrews
& Wine Antiques

A Collector's Guide

Phil Ellis

Special Consultants:
Christopher Sykes
Sally Lloyd

MILLER'S CORKSCREWS & WINE ANTIQUES:
A COLLECTOR'S GUIDE
by Phil Ellis
Special Consultants: Christopher Sykes and Sally Lloyd

First published in Great Britain in 2001 by Miller's, a division of
Mitchell Beazley, imprints of Octopus Publishing Group Ltd,
2–4 Heron Quays, London E14 4JP

Miller's is a registered trademark of Octopus Publishing Group Ltd
Copyright © Octopus Publishing Group Ltd 2001

Commissioning Editor **Anna Sanderson**
Executive Art Editor **Rhonda Fisher**
Project Editor **Emily Anderson**
Editor **Selina Mumford**
Designer **Louise Griffiths**
Proofreader **Joan Porter**
Indexer **Sue Farr**
Picture Research **Nick Wheldon**
Production **Nancy Roberts**
Jacket photography by **Steve Tanner**

ISBN 1 84000 439 8
A CIP catalogue record for this book is available from the British Library
Set in Bembo, Frutiger and Shannon
Produced by Toppan Printing Co., (HK) Ltd.
Printed and bound in China

Jacket illustrations, front cover, from top: sweet champagne bin label,
c.1840, **£220–250/$330–375**; silver-plated French tastevin, c.1900,
£40–50/$60–75; pewter "tappit hen", Scottish, c.1760, **£650–700/
$975–1,050**; champagne wire cutters with folding corkscrew, c.1870,
£260–280/$390–425 Back cover: German, gay nineties lady, legs
folding, celluloid corkscrew, c.1895, **£280–380/$460–610**
Half Title page: silver-plated wine cradle by Wiskemann, Switzerland,
c.1880, **£300–350/$480–560** Contents page: German pocket
folding Hollweg-type corkscrew, c.1900, **£70–90/$110–145**

contents

Introduction

The origin of winemaking is unknown, although legend has it that wine was accidentally discovered by a servant girl who drank some fermented grape juice which she believed to be poisonous, intending to commit suicide. She survived, and introduced the new drink to the world. We cannot know whether there is any truth in this story, but we do know that wine production dates from at least the fourth millennium BC. Wine was enjoyed by the great Middle Eastern civilizations of antiquity, including those of Egypt and Persia.

For most of its history, wine has been stored in pottery vessels or wooden casks. The Greeks and Romans used stoppered vessels, but it is assumed that the stopper was removed with the aid of a knife. Wine bottles, as we know

English "Henshall-type" corkscrew with turned bone handle and dusting brush, c.1830, **£90–120/$135–180**

them, made their first appearance in the early 17thC, but they were mostly sealed with wooden pegs wrapped in waxed linen. The use of bottles as a favoured means of storage developed with the realization that wine improved by being laid down horizontally in these smaller containers.

Corks from the Iberian Peninsula began to replace wooden pegs and were common from the mid-18thC onwards. The inventor of the corkscrew is unknown, although there are references to them dating from the 17thC. The first person to patent a corkscrew design was an English clergyman, the Reverend Samuel Henshall, in 1795. Many thousands of designs have since followed, making corkscrews a fertile field for the collector. Inventors in America, France, Germany, Ireland, Italy, Scandinavia and the United Kingdom have all made contributions of their own. Some models were highly successful, others disastrous, but all are of interest to collectors.

Some collectors are attracted to the technological developments that provided solutions to the engineering problem of extracting a cork from a bottle, while others prefer the many unusual and often amusing designs of novelty corkscrews.

Corkscrews are synonymous with wine, although corked bottles were once used for a vast array of liquids, including medicines, and the corkscrew was used to open them. Corkscrews remain the most familiar of wine-related collectables to most people, but the development of the wine trade and social customs surrounding the consumption of wine have left us with an array of objects that make fascinating collectables in their own right. The 19thC in particular has provided us with a wealth of wine-related antiques. Everything from bottles, decanter labels, barrels

Pair of carved pinewood corkscrews in the form of a cat and dog, with glass eyes, c.1930, **£15–20/$20–30**

and wine funnels to corkscrews, measures, ladles, champagne taps and coasters are collected. Some items, such as silver tastevins and neck labels, have a clear intrinsic value in addition to aesthetic and practical appeal.

Wine-related antiques are not only bought for their own sake, but as investments as well. Fortunately, however, the collector of modest means has not been priced out of the market, and it is possible to find good examples at flea markets, or even forgotten items in drawers or attics at home. This can be a very affordable area therefore, although as with most fields of collecting you can spend as much as you like. Many novice collectors start by buying indiscriminately. You should always buy what

you like, but recording and categorizing your collection where possible will help shape it into a logical and coherent whole, and this guide will help you to do this. Don't just record details of the object itself, but also the date and place where you bought it and the price you paid. In this way, you can build your own price guide that will be invaluable for future reference.

The technology of winemaking is still advancing, and social factors that influence the consumption of wine are ever-changing. Consequently, the objects associated with wine are also changing, and there are new products and new inventions coming along all the time. Therefore, the choice for the future collector can only become wider and more interesting.

Prices

Prices for antiques vary, depending particularly on the condition of the item, but also according to geographical location and market trends. The price ranges given throughout the book should be seen as a general indicator to value only. The sterling/dollar conversion has been made at a rate of £1 = $1.50 (adjust the dollar value as necessary to accord with current exchange rates).

Wine bottles

The Romans stored and exported wine in pottery Amphora holding 6gal/7pt; they also had a thriving glass industry but most of its secrets were lost with the collapse of the Empire. Until the 17thC, earthenware was the most common material for vessels used for wine. As the technology of the glass industry improved, and its products were stabilized by the use of coal in its furnaces, so glass began to take over. Glass bottles follow a clear pattern of evolution as far as their shape is concerned. Early bottles were hand blown and had a bulbous body with an indent in the base. By 1760, cylindrical bottles were being produced in one-piece moulds. The practice of "binning" or storing bottles on their sides influenced changing styles when it was realised that bottled wine improved with age.

◀ **Rare English onion-shaped wine bottle**
This bottle is typical of the "onion shape" that was ubiquitous in the late 17thC and early 18thC. These early bottles were impossible to make in a standard capacity, and the sale of wine in bottles was prohibited in England from the mid-17th until the early 19thC. Individuals, institutions and taverns often had their own bottles made, to fill from the cask or barrel in the owner's cellar. These bottles were made with seals bearing initials and sometimes a date. The three initials here represent the surname, the owner's first name and his wife's name – that is, Irving, Charles & Wynefride.

Rare English, onion-shaped, dark green glass wine bottle, c.1685, £1,200–1,400/ $1,800–2,100

▼ **Handled glass bottle**
The handle of this bottle makes it reminiscent of a decanter, and indeed wine was served from the bottle at the time. Certainly it is more likely to have been used for serving wine than for storage. While many bottles of this type were made there are few survivors, probably because they were everyday objects and handled accordingly.

Rare English, onion-shaped, black glass wine bottle, c.1690, £1,800–2,000/ $2,700–3,000

Dutch, onion-shaped, green glass wine bottle, *c.*1740,
£120–140/$180–210

▲ Dutch onion-shaped wine bottle

This fairly common Dutch example shows the onion-shaped bottle with a wider base which was less easy to knock over. Dutch "onions" are typically lighter in weight and colour than their English counterparts, and this relatively late example of the type is made of thinner glass than the earlier English bottles. Wooden pegs tied into place with string were used as seals – note the "string rim" at the top of the neck. Many of these bottles have been recovered from shipwrecks, and sometimes show signs of iridescent colouring.

▼ Nailsea glass wine pitcher

Nailsea, near Bristol in England, became famous for its glass, and the city of Bristol itself was a noted centre of the wine trade. The Nailsea glassworks was established in 1788, so this is one of its earlier pieces. The factory produced common household wares, and many of its products are typified by the speckling seen here. This was made by rolling the item onto a surface covered in blobs of white glass, absorbing them into the body.

Very large green Nailsea speckled glass wine pitcher, *c.*1790,
£270–300/$400–450

Dutch, tapered square-shaped, dark olive green Hollands gin bottle, *c.*1830,
£25–30/ $40–45

▶ Gin bottle

Just as the practice of laying down wine influenced the evolution of the bottle, so the square shape of these gin bottles was dictated by the need to pack for export. The shape enabled them to be fitted easily into a case, and they are sometimes known as "case gins" for that reason. The olive green colour was most popular, and these bottles are not uncommon.

Bin labels

As it became more widely understood that wine would improve with age by being "laid down" in bottles, so the practice of "binning" wines developed. The cork swells in contact with the wine, forming a tight seal to the bottle and helping to preserve its contents. The development of the cellar as we understand it, with its rows of bottles, created a need to keep careful records of the type of wine, when it was laid down, and so on. Wine from a given cask would be stored in a sub-division of the cellar known as a bin. The solution to the problem of identification was the bin label, which enabled the contents to be recognized at a glance. Bin labels could be made of wood, slate or even lead, but the best-known are pottery ones, and these were made by some of the leading potteries such as Spode, Wedgwood, and Minton.

▼ **Port cellar bin label**
Early bin labels such as this one were frequently made in Delftware and this example displays typically angled shoulders. The hole is where the label would have been nailed to the bin. Early Delftware labels were made in a biscuit-coloured pottery with a blueish-white glaze, and the lettering was usually in blue.

White pottery sweet champagne cellar bin label, c.1840, £220–250/$330–375

◄ **Sweet champagne cellar bin label**
This label illustrates the "coat hanger" shape into which bin labels had evolved by this time. The use of upper case letters for labels was the norm, and was intended to make them easier to see in the gloom of the cellar. Generic names were used, but occasionally they would be a little more specific, as in the case of this label. Most labels measure 10–15cm (4–6in) but some late 19thC ones are smaller.

Rare, pale green, Delft pottery port cellar bin label, c.1750, £450–480/$675–720

CHATEAU LATOUR 1851

FACT FILE

Pottery bin labels
- The name of the pottery is often found on the back, and sometimes that of the retailer.
- Look out for staining and cracks near the holes.
- Exercise caution when buying smaller, round numbered labels – it is not unknown for hotel room numbers to be passed off as these labels.

▼ **Chateau Lafite cellar bin label**

This bin label clearly identifies the contents with the chateau and vintage. These labels are particularly sought after by collectors, especially if they relate to a significant year and/or a memorable vintage. Sometimes the wording on the label is in pink lustre script such as "Bronte" or "Calcavella". Labels with the titles sherry, port, claret or madeira are common and are priced £25–£45/$40–$70 each.

White pottery dated Chateau Lafite cellar bin label, 1848, **£350–375/$525–560**

Pottery Chateau Latour label, 1851, **£350–375/$525–560**

▲ **Chateau Latour label**

Another desirable label that identifies chateau and vintage, it is notable that even for a great chateau and vintage, the label is still very plain. This tells us that the cellar is a working environment first and foremost, and the labels were designed for function. As well as classic vintages, labels for "obsolete" wines, which are no longer consumed today, are also sought after, such as "Shrub" – an old English alcoholic cordial. Labels with misspellings are popular with collectors, and are surprisingly common.

▼ **Numbered wine bin label**

This label is likely to have come from a commercial cellar. Labelling wine with numbers, which would then correspond to a ledger, was the most practical way of keeping track in a large cellar. Smaller, round numbered labels also exist and they were usually made in sets of a few dozen. They can be difficult to date with accuracy, unless made by Wedgwood, which put three letters next to the name to denote the year of manufacture.

Wedgwood, numbered bin label, 1867, **£25–30/$40–45**

Decanter & wine labels

Decanter or wine labels are sometimes known as bottle tickets, and were hung around the neck of the bottle to identify its contents. Early examples were probably no more than handwritten parchment labels, although bone, wood and ivory would also have been used. We are now most familiar with silver or silver-plated examples, hung by a chain, but enamelled labels were also popular. Some are quite plain, bearing the name of the drink and little else, others are much more elaborate, and thousands of designs were produced. Manufacture of labels in Britain was severely curtailed as a result of legislation passed in 1860, which decreed that wine merchants would have to paper-label their bottles before sale, making wine labels largely obsolete except for decanter labels.

◀ **Polychrome enamel decanter label**
Staffordshire, and most notably the town of Bilston, was the major centre of enamelling in England in the late 18thC. Battersea in London was also a centre of production, but Battersea labels tended to be transfer printed rather than painted. The Staffordshire factories turned out a wide variety of small enamelled wares, in addition to these labels. The Samson French factory, c.1920, also produced wine, perfume and sauce labels with chains.

Staffordshire enamel port decanter label, c.1780, **£250–280/ $375–420**

▼ **Silver wine label**
While most wine labels have the names of the wine already marked on them in some way (usually engraved), this label is unusual in that it allows the user to change the name to suit the drink being served. The name is displayed in a small window on a vellum ticket which can be replaced via an opening at the back of the label. This crescent-shaped wine label depicts a gentleman carving a sturgeon – not the most common of motifs.

Continental silver wine label, c.1810, **£240–260/ $360–390**

▲ **Silver-plated gin
decanter label**
This is a comparatively late
example. Collectors can choose
from "G" for gin, "P" for port,
"S" for sherry and so on.
These decanter labels can
be inexpensive and there
are many different variations
in size and style. They can
also be used to personalize
decanters if you share an
initial. While some of these
labels date from as early as
the 18thC, they were especially
popular between about the
1830s and 1870s, when most
of them were made. Generally
the more decorative they are,
the better. Scottish examples
tend to be comparatively plain.

▼ **Silver sherry label**
Until 1790, neck labels and
other small items of silver did
not have to be hallmarked
and dating them can therefore
prove difficult. Some bear no
marks whatsoever, although
many do have a maker's
mark. This can be a valuable
indication of an approximate
date, otherwise it is necessary
to rely on studying styles and
designs of a given period.

Silver, Xeres (sherry) label,
unmarked, c.1775,
£100–120/$150–180

Silver (hallmarked) Moselle label,
by J. Barber and W. North, York,
1845, **£170–190/$250–285**

▲ **Silver Moselle label**
York is one of the provincial
English assay offices that is no
longer in operation: it closed
its doors in 1857. Hallmarks
of unusual cities, such as
York, Hull and Chester, fetch
better prices than London,
Birmingham and Sheffield.

Silver gin label,
by John Reily, London,
1811, **£70–90/$100–135**

▼ Silver brandy label

Silver labels of the late 18thC were fairly small and discreet. Thin, lightweight labels were the norm – note the curved shape, which is designed to fit snugly around the neck of the bottle or decanter. The popularity of coloured decanters for spirits in the late 18thC would have made labels such as this all the more useful as an aid to identifying the contents, although these decanters often bore names of drink in gilt lettering.

Silver brandy label, by Matthew Linwood, Birmingham, 1781, **£90–110/$135–165**

▲ Silver gin label

In the late 18thC, coloured decanters bearing the name of the beverage were a frequent fixture at the dining table. As cut-glass decanters became more popular, so the decanter label came into its own for a range of drinks. This decorative label with a border showing juniper berries and leaves alludes to the drink in the same way as does the fashion for vine leaf motifs on wine labels.

▼ Set of silver spirits labels

The labels of the Victorian era grew more elaborate as it became possible to produce ever more fanciful designs for a lower cost. The lack of markings on labels can be expected to have an adverse affect on the price, but as a set they become more valuable. Rather than showing a variation on the familiar vine leaf motifs, they are decorated with cornucopia, sheaves of corn and farming tools, and named "Free Trade", linking the set to a political controversy of the era. This gives it an additional historical interest that combines with the other factors mentioned to make this a desirable acquisition.

Unmarked silver labels, c.1840, **£550–600/$825–900 the set**

▼ **Silver port label**

The single vine leaf became
a very popular form for wine
labels in the mid 19thC.
They come in various sizes
and weights and differing
quality, and the majority
were simply stamped from a
sheet of metal. The large-scale
manufacture of such labels
became possible as metal-
working technology advanced.

Victorian silver vine leaf port
label, by Yapp & Woodward,
Birmingham, 1853,
£70–80/$100–120

Silver-plated pair of sherry and
madeira labels, English, c.1930,
£12–15/$18–22 each

▲ **Silver-plated sherry
and madeira labels**

These labels are quite plain,
a factor that affects the price
since decorative labels are
generally more popular.
They are plated, and as
20thC pieces would have
been electroplated rather than
Sheffield plated, the latter is
more popular with collectors.

▼ **Cast silver whisky label**

This large and heavy piece
was made to commemorate
the accession to the throne
of Queen Elizabeth II. It is
stamped with the maker's
mark "LGD" and bears the
royal lions and crown; it
has an additional value as a
commemorative piece. Whisky
labels from earlier years
can be quite rare for social
reasons: in the 18thC it was
not considered a gentleman's
drink, and was consumed
primarily by those unable
to afford silver labels.

Cast silver whisky label, London,
1953, **£130–150/$195–225**

Pewter measures

Pewter is an alloy of tin and varying proportions of other metals such as antimony and zinc. It is known to have existed in ancient times, but surviving specimens are rare before the 17th and 18thC. Part of the reason for this is that the metal has a low melting point, so it was easy to produce new items from old ones that had either been damaged, or had simply gone out of fashion. In England, its manufacture was regulated by the Pewterers' Company from the mid 15thC. Makers meeting the required standards could register a mark or "touch" to be used on their products. Pewter had many uses for the innkeeper, the best known being as drinking vessels. It was the material of choice because it does not break, unlike pottery and glass containers. It was also used for measures.

German, pewter lidded wine stein, 1674, **£650–700/ $975–1,050**

◀ **Lidded wine stein**
This pewter piece bears the Arms of the Haberdashers Guild, and an inscription in German. Attached to the base of the tankard is a second base, which contains a wooden dice visible through a series of holes. When the tankard has been drained, it can then be turned upside down and used for dice games – quite possibly to determine who would pay for the drinks! The coat of arms suggests that it would have been especially appropriate for social occasions such as guild dinners.

▼ **"Tappit hen"**
The "tappit hen" is a Scottish measure whose capacity is equivalent to 60floz (3 pints), and is therefore one of the larger measures commonly encountered. This piece displays the "tappit" (top knot) and flared mouth, or "beak", that give it its distinctive name. The shape makes it particularly interesting, and it would be a desirable addition to any collection as a good example of the type.

Pewter "tappit hen", c.1760, **£650–700/ $975–1,050**

▼ **Pewter lidded flagon**

This piece was made by George Maxwell of Glasgow, who is recognized as one of the best makers in this field. The price of this flagon reflects both the quality of the piece and the reputation of the maker. Added interest is always provided by additional marks and inscriptions, and this piece does not disappoint: the base is marked with a ship and the patriotic inscription "Success to the British Colonies".

Scottish, large pewter lidded flagon, c.1780, **£1,700–1,800/ $2,550–2,700**

English, half gill measure, c.1790, **£120–140/$180–210**

▲ **18thC half gill measure**

Decorative appeal is added to this measure by the double volute (twisted or spiral decoration) on the lid. It is of baluster shape, and its half gill capacity would have been useful for spirits. In England, measures used in inns and taverns were (and are) strictly regulated. Establishments would receive regular visits from officials who would check the measures to ensure that they conformed to set standards. Sets of measures of varying capacity were used, and collectors are especially keen to acquire a complete set.

▼ **19thC half gill measure**

This "belly"-shaped tavern measure was used for spirits. It is stamped to the left of the handle on the rim with "half gill" and a Victorian Weights and Measures inspector's mark of "VR 239 LCC". The measure is engraved with the name of the tavern from where it originally came. Measures that can be traced to a specific tavern are always more desirable than those that are anonymous.

English, half gill measure, c.1870, **£20–25/$30–40**

Testing & measuring

The testing of wines and spirits for quantity and/or alcoholic content was, and is, essential to the trade, and to the taxman. Some examples of instruments used for such purposes are shown here. The invention of the slide rule is generally credited to the Reverend William Oughtred in around 1630, though the earliest surviving examples date from the mid 17thC. By the end of the century, the rules were being designed specifically for the measurement of the contents of containers by excise officers. The hydrometer was invented by Robert Boyle in the 17thC, and measures the specific gravity of liquids, enabling alcoholic strength to be calculated. Some of these instruments were used by professionals at vintners, or by customs officers, while others were used by staff working in an inn or tavern.

◀ **Boxwood slide rule**
This instrument is made of boxwood, a popular material for use in the manufacture of slide rules. As a very dense wood, it is particularly resistant to the problems of expansion and contraction caused by changes in humidity, to which softer woods are susceptible. This rule therefore runs smoothly and can be read accurately – a stable material is essential when making any precision instrument. Leading manu-facturer Edward Roberts made this example.

Four-sided wine merchants' slide rule, 1759–1769, **£120–140/ $180–210**

▼ **18thC slide rules**
While boxwood was an excellent choice of material for a testing rule, ivory was an even better one. It is still more stable than boxwood, and less liable to suffer from variations in humidity. Ivory was used for general purpose slide rules, not just for those connected with the wine trade, and this one was for calculating the proof of spirits, while the boxwood rule was for testing the gravity of wine barrels. Both were made by John Long, one of the better-known makers in this field.

Slide rules.
Top: ivory,
1781–1811,
£130–150/ $200–225;
bottom:
boxwood,
c.1790,
£60–80/ $90–120

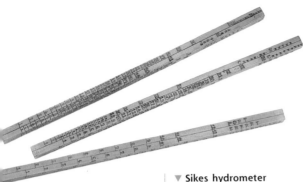

Three boxwood four-sided rules, 1890, **£80–90/$120–135**

▲ **A set of four-sided rules**
These rules were designed to give an indication of how many measures of wine or spirits remained in the bottle. The rule was simply held against the bottle by bar staff, and the number of drinks remaining could be seen at a glance. There are different scales, which can be read according to whether the bottle contains rum, whisky, brandy or so on.

▼ **Sikes hydrometer**
This Sikes hydrometer, made by J. Long, comprises a gilt brass ball with a rod passing through its centre, to which gilt circular weights can be attached. The ball will sink or float to a level dependent on the density, or specific gravity, of the liquid; the proportion of alcohol present can thereby be calculated. There were various versions of the hydrometer, but the Sikes, introduced in the 19thC, was considered the most effective.

Sikes hydrometer, c.1890, **£80–90/$120–135**

String dispenser, c.1860, **£125–150/$190–225**

▲ **String dispenser**
While it has no practical connection with the wine trade, items such as this are popular with collectors of wine-related antiques. It was designed purely as a novelty string dispenser; the ball of string is contained within the barrel and emerges from the tap. The wine barrel was always a popular form of container for various purposes.

Ladles & funnels

The first funnels appeared around the mid 17thC and early examples are rare, and generally quite plain. There are many surviving funnels from the late 18thC onwards, and these are often decorative. The most common materials used were silver, silver plate and pewter, with glass and porcelain examples being rare. Many ladles have a silver coin inset into the bottom of the bowl and the date of the coin is sometimes the date of the ladle. Funnels were mainly used for decanting wine and port into decanters ready for the table. Silver and glass wine funnels always had a slight curve at the bottom of the spout, so that when the wine was being decanted it would pour gently against the inside of the decanter. Punch was hugely popular in the 17th and 18thC, and consequently much of the paraphernalia surrounding it has survived, including bowls and ladles.

◀ **Silver and fruitwood punch ladle**
Many early punch ladles were made entirely of wood, but by this time silver was the preferred material for quality pieces. Nevertheless, the use of wood survives in the fruitwood handle of this ladle. (Lignum vitae was also used for making handles.) The ladle is quite deep and fairly elaborate in design, probably in keeping with the punchbowl that would originally have gone with it.

Silver punch ladle, London, 1774, **£185–200/$280–300**

Silver punch ladle, London, 1790, **£125–145/$190–220**

▶ **Silver and whalebone punch ladle**
This ladle has a handle of whalebone, which was a very popular material for such purposes from about the middle of the 18thC onwards. It is a fairly easy material to work with and to manipulate into useful shapes. The twist of this handle is designed to give an easier grip to the user. Towards the end of the century the bowl of the ladle became shallower and broader.

Silver wine funnels
These were often made in one piece but some were made in several pieces, which could then be dismantled. The main reason for this was for cleaning the funnel, but also for allowing a fine piece of muslin to be put between the spout and the straining bowl for extra fine filtering. Each component should bear a separate hallmark.

Silver wine funnel, by J. McKay, Edinburgh, c.1826, £850–950/$1,275–1,425

▼ Sheffield plate funnel

In spite of its name Sheffield plate does not automatically come from Sheffield, since the term is a generic one. Birmingham as well as Sheffield was a major centre of its production. The process of making Sheffield plate was made obsolete by electroplating, which was invented in 1840. Until then, many objects that would have been made in silver were made in Sheffield plate and a large number have survived. The price reflects this.

Sheffield plate wine funnel, c.1820, £80–90/$120–135

▲ Silver wine funnel

Scotland has enjoyed a long and illustrious history of silversmithing, and Scottish silver is a collecting field in its own right. While early wine funnels were quite plain, later ones were more decorative. The most obvious scope for decoration on such an object is the rim, which is more elaborate than the simpler gadrooning (decorative pattern of curved flutings) of the Sheffield plate example (see below left). Note also the strainer that removes bits of sediment and perhaps cork from the wine as it is decanted.

▶ Silver toddy ladle

Toddy is generally a stronger drink than punch, which is why a toddy ladle is much smaller than its punch equivalent. The silver bowls of some of the early toddy ladles were formed from silver coins, which were beaten into the shape of the bowl. On some examples the edge of the bowl has the wording of the coin's edge clearly visible. Unmarked silver can still be quite collectable, but marked pieces will always be more desirable.

Silver toddy ladle, unmarked, Scottish, c.1880, £30–35/ $45–55

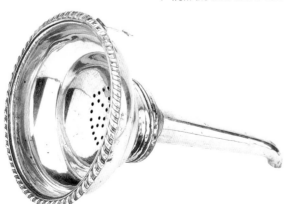

Cradles & bottle holders

Although the serving of wine in decanters, rather than straight from the bottle, became the norm in the 19thC, there were certain wines that were regarded as the exception and should only be served from the bottle. Whether this is mere wine snobbery or if it really is significant is a matter of opinion, but suitable equipment to allow for the serving of wine in this way developed nonetheless. Keeping a bottle of wine at an angle allowed any sediment to settle out of harm's way, and made it possible for the wine to be poured with a minimum of disturbance. Some wine cradles feature a mechanism that allows the bottle to be tilted slowly and gently. With most modern wines there is unlikely to be a problem with sediment, but with older wines a cradle such as this can be a useful accessory.

Nailsea pale green glass wine funnel holder, c.1840,
£80–90/ $120–135

▶ **Nailsea glass wine funnel holder**
This whimsical piece is typical of Nailsea glass, which is associated with domestic items of all kinds as well as novelty items such as rolling pins, glass ships, and bells. This decorative, yet functional, piece overlaps collecting fields, and would be as much prized by a glass collector as an example of its type, as by a wine enthusiast.

▼ **Silver-plated sleigh-shaped bottle cradle**
Wine cradles were particularly abundant in the late 19thC. The necessary shape required for its function suggested several things in the minds of the designers. Here, the designer has taken a sleigh as inspiration; a cannon was another popular choice. While there is no ring to hold the bottle neck, the flexible metal on which the neck rests could also have acted as a kind of clamp to help secure it.

Silver-plated wine cradle, by Wiskemann, Swiss, c.1880,
£300–350/$450–525

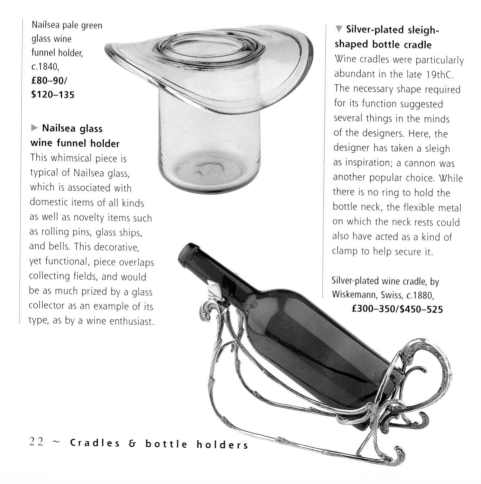

FACT FILE

Wood or metal?
• Early 19thC English decanting machines are usually made of mahogany, not metal.
• Many French decanting machines are made of steel or iron.
• The more sophisticated mechanical models are especially sought after, but must be in good working order to fetch top prices.

Silver-plated bottle cradle, by Hukin & Heath, c.1881, **£1,500–1,700/$2,250–2,550**

▲ **Silver-plated bottle cradle**
A stylishly designed piece, the ebony handle facilitates pouring and the loop at the front for slipping over the neck prevents the bottle from sliding forward when in use. The three wide circular bands that form the cradle are held together by silver-plated bars. This piece was made by Hukin & Heath, who manufactured the work of the renowned designer Christopher Dresser. Although it does not bear Dresser's mark, there is a good chance that this piece is one of his designs.

▼ **Adjustable wire bottle cradle**
The vast majority of bottle cradles were silver plated, as is this attractive example which is made from plated thick wire. The bottle sits in its "cage" and is held in position by a loop, which slides down the neck of the bottle. The "cage" rests in the shaped base, and can be gently tilted to pour the wine.

Silver-plated adjustable wire bottle cradle, French, c.1900, **£150–200/$225–300**

Bottle cradle, English, c.1980, **£200–250/$300–375**

▲ **Mechanical bottle cradle**
This copy of an earlier design is made of brass and stands on a mahogany base. The mechanism is straightforward, and one of various different types used. The mechanical cradle has been reproduced in fair numbers, partly because originals can sell for large sums and are hard to come by. When they do appear, many are badly worn.

Coasters & tastevins

As the rituals and formalities of dining developed, so too did the accessories associated with it. Coasters appeared as a regular feature of the dining table from the 1760s. They were made in pairs or sets and never entirely of silver, as the bases were always of wood. The sides of the coasters helped to prevent decanters from being knocked against each other, causing chips or cracks. Tastevins or "tasters", as their name suggests, were designed for sampling small quantities of wine; a professional tool for use by vintners, examples are known from the 16thC although they were certainly used well before then. Apart from being functional, tastevins can also be quite decorative and offer excellent opportunities for the silver collector as well as the wine enthusiast.

Sheffield plate decanter coaster, c.1830, **£120–150/ $180–225**

▲ Decanter coaster
In the 19thC Sheffield plate became the preferred material for many wine accessories formerly made in silver, including coasters. By about 1850, coasters in solid silver had become rare. This coaster, with its turned out gadrooned rim, is typical of the Regency style. It also has a central boss on the base, which would sometimes bear the coat of arms of its owner.

▼ Table decanter wagon
The decanter wagon was a more elaborate and amusing way of serving wine than plain coasters. This is essentially two coasters joined together, the wheels allowing easier passage at the larger, formal dinner parties that had become popular by this time. Its cranked pulling handle attached to a fixed axle allows the wagon to travel in a circle. Early examples have their wheels hidden, and wagons with exposed wheels, such as this, date from the 19thC.

Sheffield plate table decanter wagon with turned walnut bases, c.1830, **£1,500–1,600/ $2,250–2,400**

FACT FILE

- Early wooden bases of coasters were made of mahogany, lignum vitae, or rosewood.
- Pairs or sets of coasters are much more valuable than individual items.
- French tastevins come in two styles – the Burgundy style is cup-shaped, while the Bordeaux style is more of a shallow cone.

French, silver-plated tastevin, c.1900, **£40–50/$60–75**

▼ Miniature silver tastevin

As with punch ladles (see pp.20–21), coins were some-times inset into the base of tastevins; the coin in this example dates it to 1872. As one might expect, these objects were particularly numerous in France and other Continental wine-producing countries. Many English tastevins were made, based on French designs, and examples do survive, but they are few in numbers after about 1750.

Miniature silver tastevin, French, with a chain for wearing round the neck, 1872, **£450–500/$675–750**

▲ Silver-plated tastevin

Tastevins are generally rarer than objects such as coasters, because they were used by a limited number of people in the wine trade, rather than by the wine-drinking public. They generally have a raised centre and were used to assess the colour and clarity of the wine, as well as its taste. Silver's reflective properties aided this inspection and make it the material of choice for tastevins over others such as porcelain.

Silver-plated wine bottle coaster, c.1930, **£25–30/$40–45**

▲ Wine bottle coaster

The manufacture of coasters appears to have died out at the end of the 19thC, apart from reproductions. The plain, streamlined design of this piece is in keeping with the Art Deco era in which it was made.

Tantalus & decanters

Tantalus was a character from Greek mythology, who was punished by the gods. He was forced to stand up to his neck in water with fruits hanging over him. The water receded when he tried to drink, while the fruit was blown out of reach when he tried to eat. It is from his name that we get the word "tantalize" and the name of lockable containers for decanters. A locked case would certainly "tantalize" the keyless would-be drinker, and thwart servants such as the butler. Decanters date from the latter part of the 17thC, although the distinction between decanters and bottles is blurred at this time. Serving wine from a decanter rather than from a bottle was partly practical – sediment from the bottle could be removed before serving. However, it was also very much a question of fashion, and by the 19thC the use of decanters was widespread.

Georgian cut and engraved port decanter, coat of arms, c.1810, **£850–950/ $1,275–1,425**

▶ **Georgian port decanter**
Port had become a hugely popular drink in England at this time, partly because French wines were not generally available owing to the Napoleonic wars. The step-cut neck of this decanter would have helped the server to maintain a firm grip, while the mushroom-shaped stopper is consistent with decanters made between 1800 and 1820. The engraved armorial adds interest to this piece.

▼ **Cut-glass decanters**
The style of the sherry decanter (below right) is one of the earlier forms dating from the 17thC. The Victorians were noted for reviving the earlier styles, and decanters are no exception. By the late 19thC, the shape of decanters was generally dictated by the drink to be served from it, and the square shape of the decanter on the left marks it out for spirits.

Below right: Victorian sherry decanter, c.1850, **£170–190/ $255–285**; below left: spirit decanter, c.1890, **£60–80/ $90–120**

Tantalus with silver-plated frame and three cut-glass decanters, c.1890, **£600–650/$900–975**

▼ Oak tantalus
The front of this tantalus unlocks and hinged flaps on the top fold outwards allowing access to the contents. As well as the decanters, the box would have space for glasses and/or cigars, and the contents might also include cards, dominoes, draughts and a cribbage board.

Victorian, carved oak three-bottle tantalus with nickel mounts, c.1890, **£750–850/ $1,125–1,275**

▲ Tantalus with silver-plated frame
The decanters above are of the typical square form with a globe stopper that was popular for spirits at the time. This "open frame" tantalus recalls the earlier styles that were much in use before c.1850, which was when the more elaborate boxes started to make their appearance. This tantalus is locked at the top, the frame preventing removal of the decanters.

▼ Pewter claret jug
Glass claret jugs with silver or other metal mounts date from the early 19thC, and during the Art Nouveau and Art Deco periods designers used them as a vehicle for exploring amusing or whimsical design ideas. This design is typical of that style – not only ducks but other animals, mainly birds, provided inspiration, and the claret jug comes in a multitude of styles.

Art Deco-style, duck-shaped pewter claret jug, Etain Du Manoir, French, c.1960, **£180–200/$270–300**

Champagne taps & wire cutters

Champagne is the name of a French wine-producing region and, although it is sometimes used as a generic term for sparkling wines, only those from this region can strictly be called champagne. Today, we associate champagne with celebration, but this wasn't always the case. It was originally considered to be a health drink, and was even prescribed by doctors. It was believed to be particularly beneficial as a tonic to pregnant women and nursing mothers. The champagne tap, which allowed small quantities of the drink to be drawn from the bottle without uncorking it, was therefore a useful device. Since champagne is sadly no longer available on prescription, most bottles are drunk in one go at social occasions and the tap is a device that has now passed into the history books.

◄ **Silver-plated "Prince of Wales" tap**

S. Maw & Son of London, who made this piece, also made medical instruments, which provides another indication that champagne was indeed thought to have health-giving properties (see above). This example is widely referred to as a "soda water tap" suggesting suitability for fizzy drinks other than champagne. It is quite decorative, comes in an attractive leather case, and gets its name from the plumes of feathers which form the on/off turns: these feathers have been the traditional symbol of the Prince of Wales for many years.

Silver-plated "Prince of Wales"-tap, c.1890, **£80–90/ $120–135**

▼ **Trocar spikes**

W. Ryder patented the model with the turned ebony handle (right) in 1874. It uses a trocar spike inside a tube known as an Abyssinian tap. The stopper is penetrated by the spike, then the handle unscrews from the tap to allow the spike to be removed and the champagne to flow through the tube. The nickel-plated example (left) is inserted in much the same way as a corkscrew.

Right: trocar spike, c.1890, **£70–80/ $105–120**; left: finger ring trocar spike, c.1890, **£170–190/$255–285**

▼ Wire cutters

Many tools of the champagne trade are sought after by collectors. These cutters were used to tackle the wire fastening the cork to the bottle and were (and are) extremely useful to have around the cellar. Both are fitted with the dusting brushes that were so handy for clearing away the debris around the neck of the bottle. The silver-plated example (left) still has its original box, which adds to the value, and the inclusion of a corkscrew on the other cutter is also a very desirable feature. Wire cutters of this type rarely incorporate corkscrews.

Left: silver-plated wire cutters, c.1900, **£140–170/$210–255**; right: wire cutters with corkscrew, c.1870, **£260–280/$390–420**

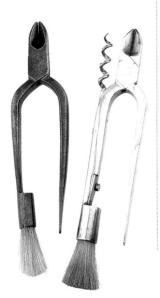

Nickel-plated champagne tap in leather case, c.1900, **£60–75/$90–115**

▲ Nickel-plated tap

The notion of champagne as a restorative was especially popular in the last quarter of the 19thC and into the early 20th, so this piece was made at the height of this fashion. It is of the "detachable spike" type and comes with two spikes. It is simple to operate; the tap is inserted completely through the cork of the unopened bottle, and a spike at the end falls into the bottom of the bottle, allowing the liquid to flow through the tap. After the champagne has been consumed the spike can be removed from the bottle for re-use.

▼ Nickel-plated tap

As with corkscrews, makers often gave their champagne taps impressive-sounding names, designed to instil confidence. This model, known as "The Champion", was made by James Heeley & Sons. Complete with its original green card box, it is stamped on the on/off turn "RD 253107 J. H. & S", indicating the maker and the registration number for the year 1926.

Nickel-plated champagne tap with rubber bung, 1926, **£150–170/$225–255**

Cork inserters & bar cork drawers

Here, we see a selection of items designed to insert and withdraw corks; both are connected with the trade. In England during the second half of the 19thC, and particularly towards the end of the century, pubs and bars as we know them today began to emerge. Rising living standards and changing social customs placed greater emphasis on them as a place for socializing and entertainment. This meant that there was a need for bar staff to be able to serve more people, more quickly. The result was the development of bar cork drawers that could insert a worm, withdraw a cork and eject it again quickly and efficiently with the turn of a handle. Also shown here are cork inserters, which have long been essential to the wine trade. They are sometimes overlooked, but make interesting additions to a wine antiques collection.

▼ **19thC bar cork drawer**
This model is known as "The Eclipse", and has a revolving ash handle. The supporting column is engraved "Eclipse" with a sunrise trade mark. Its circular base has countersunk screws, enabling it to be screwed into the top of the bar. This piece is in working order, and features a left-handed "speed worm" (see p.62).

Brass bar cork drawer, c.1890, **£750–800/ $1,125– 1,200**

Wine bottler's corking tool, c.1900, **£30–35/£45–55**

▶ **Cork inserter**
This is a tool designed to insert, rather than withdraw, corks, but like the bar cork drawers it was designed with professional use in mind. This example is of turned walnut and is operated by hand. With the plunger raised, the cork is placed into the chamber. When the plunger is depressed the cork is squeezed out of the aperture at the end, which is very slightly narrower than the neck of a wine bottle. When positioned against the top of a bottle the cork will be forced into the neck, where it will expand again for a snug fit.

Cast steel bar cork drawer, c.1910, **£120–140/ $180–210**

▲ Cast steel bar cork drawer

This impressive piece of engineering is named "The Original Safety". It was patented in the USA by Gilchrist, but was manufactured in England by Gaskell & Chambers from 1894. It is attractively decorated, and features a clamp for securing it to any bar with an overhanging edge. Solid and heavy, its side panels are cast with the words "Original Safety Trademark Reg No 543083" and "Made in England". It is 25cm (10in) high, and in perfect working order.

▼ French cork inserter

This cork inserter is made of sycamore. It features iron bands, which gave the body additional strength to withstand the rigours of regular use. These cork inserters are not always easy to operate, at least for the uninitiated, but they were certainly in widespread use and are readily available. The plunger in this case is reinforced with a tin cap.

Brass bar cork drawer, c.1920, **£280–300/ $420–450**

▲ 20thC bar cork drawer

This is a fine example of what was undoubtedly one of the most successful bar cork drawer designs. Known as "The Don", it was patented in 1903, although this one dates from around 1920. It was made by Gaskell & Chambers, who dominated the market in England at this time producing four bar cork drawer patents, of which this was one. It has a brass body and an ash operating handle.

Sycamore cork inserter, French, c.1920, **£35–40/$55–60**

Thomasons & barrel corkscrews

In the late 17thC when corks were first used, they were not driven all the way home into the neck of the bottle – instead the cork protruded for easier opening. From the 18thC it became common practice for corks to be driven flush with the neck of the bottle, thereafter making corkscrews essential. The Thomason corkscrew was the first major corkscrew patent of the 19thC, being patented in 1802 by Edward Thomason. The worm was enclosed in a barrel, and it used an ingenious hermaphrodite screw (see p.62) to remove the cork from the bottle and eject it from the corkscrew. Thomason was a prolific inventor and manufacturer, and was knighted in 1832. Many barrel and Thomason-type corkscrews have remained in production long after they first appeared – a tribute to their fine design.

◄ The "King's Screw"
In spite of its name, the "King's Screw" has no connection with royalty, and the origin of the name is unclear, though it may be a reference to its superior performance. The "King's Screw" uses a rack and pinion mechanism to extract the cork, hence the second handle at the side. The cork is extracted without being turned in the process. This corkscrew has an "open frame" design rather than enclosing the worm completely in a barrel and a turned bone handle with detachable brush end.

Silver-plated, four-pillar "King's Screw", c.1820, **£550–650/ $825–975**

▼ Lund with bronze barrel
The name of Lund is to be found on many of the more ingenious mechanical corkscrews. The sprung sheet steel grips hold the bottle securely in place and it employs a rack and pinion mechanism for extraction. The use of bronze for the barrel was quite typical of these corkscrews at this time. The firm of Lund is one of the most famous in corkscrew manufacture. It was founded by Thomas Lund in the mid 19thC and patented numerous different designs. One of the firm's many successful products was a comparatively inexpensive version of the King's screw, which was known as the "London Rack".

Rare, Lund, patent bronze barrel, bottle grips marked "Lund London patentee", 1838, **£3,000–4,000/ $4,500–6,000**

▼ Double-action "King's Screw"

Bone, as well as wood, was a popular material for the handles of corkscrews like this one. The cork is pierced and extracted by turning the handle in one direction. This type of corkscrew is very well designed and always runs smoothly. Collectors like to find good corkscrews in working order and this style seldom disappoints, hence its popularity and value. Dowler, who is credited with the patent, worked with Thomason and is one of the best-known names.

Brass, wide rack "King's Screw" with "Dowler patent" tablet (maker's name badge), c.1820, **£650–750/$975–1,125**

Left: bronze barrel, Thomason-type with turned bone handle, c.1810, **£1,000–1,200/$1,500–1,800**; right: brass, double-action Thomason-type, with half round "Royal Arms" tablet, c.1850, **£275–300/$415–450**

▲ Decorative corkscrews

While some Thomason-type corkscrews have plain barrels, this example (left) is embossed with fruit. As well as the decoration shown here, a Gothic-style church window was another popular design. Such decoration adds to the appeal of a corkscrew. The brass example (right) is also decorated, but with a coat of arms. It has a split ring for hanging, and like many corkscrews includes a dusting brush. This brush was used for removing any bits of sealing wax and other debris from around the neck of the bottle and for dusting off paper wine labels.

▼ 20thC Italian corkscrew

Quite apart from its usefulness as a corkscrew, this 20thC Italian piece has great novelty value, making it popular with many collectors, yet it remains quite affordable. The cork is simply pierced by turning the head of the figure, a moustached sommelier, while the arms give good leverage to assist the extraction of the cork.

Silver-plated, Italian, two-lever barrel, c.1960, **£35–45/$55–70**

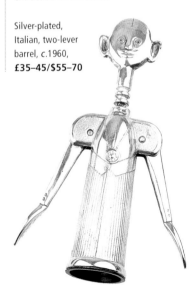

Corkscrews: small & portable

Pocket corkscrews were known from around the mid 18thC and there were many reasons why they were desirable – for use on picnics, for example. Today, corkscrews are used almost exclusively for uncorking bottles of wine, but this was not always the case. Many were designed with ladies in mind and were used to open perfume bottles, as well as medicine bottles. Corkscrews of the peg and worm type (see p.62), or serpentine screws as they are sometimes known in the USA, date back to the 18thC and were made throughout the 19thC and into the 20thC. Most corkscrews were designed for function and were made of simple materials, but silver pocket corkscrews were made in considerable numbers from the late 18thC onwards, with the worm generally housed in a sheath.

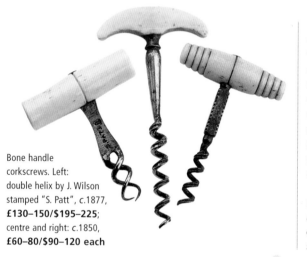

Bone handle corkscrews. Left: double helix by J. Wilson stamped "S. Patt", c.1877, **£130–150/$195–225**; centre and right: c.1850, **£60–80/$90–120 each**

▼ **English miniatures with bone handles**
The spring assisted corkscrew was especially popular in Germany and France, but was also made in England. As the worm penetrates the cork, so the spring on the shank begins to exert force, making its removal easier. Note the different types of worm used.

Right: open-frame, spring-assisted, c.1880, **£80–90/$120–135**; centre: c.1840; left: c.1880, **£70–90/$105–135 each**

▲ **English miniatures**
These are much sought after by collectors, partly because there are still quite a lot of them around, and they are available in a wide range of styles. Most had a single helical worm, but some have a double helix, as in the example seen here.

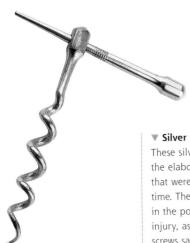

Victorian, left-handed peg and worm corkscrew, c.1860, **£120–150/$180–225**

▲ Gilded steel peg and worm corkscrew

The peg and worm corkscrew consists of two pieces (see p.62). Comparatively few of these corkscrews have survived, probably because it was so easy to lose the parts. Intriguingly many of these corkscrews were made with a left-hand thread, but the reason for this is unclear.

▼ Silver pocket corkscrews

These silver corkscrews feature the elaborate decorative styles that were quite popular at the time. They can be easily carried in the pocket without risk of injury, as the worm simply screws safely into the sheath provided. They also incorporate other useful gadgets such as pipe tampers, while the ends could be used as wax seals. As well as these silver-handled examples, some have handles made from other materials: mother-of-pearl was a popular choice and there are occasional ivory-handled ones.

Dutch, silver pocket corkscrews, c.1850, **£800–1,000/ $1,200–1,500 each**

Birmingham, silver-sheathed corkscrews, c.1790–1810, **£400–500/$600–750 each**

▲ Silver-sheathed corkscrews

Birmingham was responsible for a great many of these silver sheathed corkscrews, produced by makers such as Willmore and Pemberton. The use of ivory for handles, as on these corkscrews, is quite rare, and more common bone-handled examples may be mistaken for ivory by novice collectors.

Novelty corkscrews

Novelty corkscrews might seem trivial, but they are certainly amusing and must have started many a collector on the road to corkscrew addiction. As well as extracting the cork, the necessary functions of a novelty corkscrew are also adapted to give an entertaining effect. Corkscrews were originally manufactured purely for their function, but as living standards rose there was more of a demand for these novelty pieces. The increasing availability and consumption of wine no doubt helped to boost the popularity of corkscrews of all types. At the end of the 19thC, the "naughty nineties" inspired and allowed novelty corkscrews of a more risqué nature. Many of these were Continental in make. It should not be assumed that all novelty corkscrews were limited in their functionality – many were quite sturdy and extremely useful.

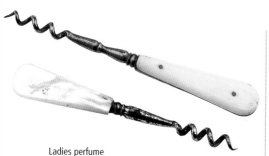

Ladies perfume or medicine bottle corkscrews, c.1870, **£18–28/ $28–42 each**

▲ English perfume or medicine bottle corkscrews
The handles of these bottle corkscrews were frequently made of bone or mother-of-pearl, and occasionally ivory. Their form suggests that they would have been used for opening perfume or medicine bottles, but also small bottles of spirits or liqueurs carried "for medicinal purposes". They are widely available and affordable, and therefore make ideal purchases for those just starting a collection.

▼ Ladies' legs
These pocket corkscrews were made in various sizes and stocking colour combinations, some striped and others plain. Because of this variety and their amusing design, they have captured the imagination of today's collectors. The legs, when folded, cover the worm while travelling and also act as levers when the cork is drawn. The inspiration, of course, comes from the Can Can dancers of Paris.

German, gay nineties ladies' legs, folding, celluloid corkscrews, c.1895, **£280–380/ $420–570 each**

German, folding pocket corkscrews. Left: depicts "wood shoes", c.1900, **£280–320/ $420–480**; right: depicts nickel-plated horse's legs, 1909, **£350–400/$525–600**

▲ **Folding pocket corkscrews**
German makers in particular showed an impressive flair for design and considerable imagination. These two corkscrews show examples of different types of worm. The "wood shoes" (left) has a flat bladed worm, while the horse's legs example has a helical worm. The latter also incorporates a useful wire cutter, and both are stamped "DRGM". These letters stand for "Deutsches Reichs Gebrauchsmuster", which translates as "German state patent" and is only found on pre-1918 corkscrews.

German, mermaid corkscrew, c.1900, **£700–900/ $1,050–1,350**

▼ **Mermaid corkscrew**
This novelty corkscrew is something of a rarity, and has other useful features besides a cork extractor. This example has a cap lifter, as well as a foil cutter for peeling off the foil or just slicing it through for removal. This piece is marked "Ges. Geschutzt", an abbreviation for "Gesetzlich Geschützt", which means "protected by patent". Variations on this type may be found in different finishes, with or without a foil cutter.

English, pocket corkscrew with ivory sheath, c.1850, **£170–200/ $255–300**

▲ **English pocket corkscrew**
Like the peg and worm examples (see pp.34–35), this corkscrew is in two pieces. However, in this case the handle is removed to form the sheath into which the worm can be screwed for safe travelling. While this one has an ivory sheath, corkscrews of this type more commonly have steel sheaths. They were designed for use on picnics or when on a journey.

Corkscrews: all steel

The "cellarmans" corkscrews might, at first glance, seem to have limited appeal to the collector. They are certainly plain, and these functional, very simple, steel corkscrews, whose use would have been confined to the cellar, lack the sheer decorative appeal or complexity of operation that distinguishes many other types. Nevertheless, they are among the most affordable of corkscrews and this factor alone is enough to endear them to many collectors. There is still sufficient variation in design to make them an attractive proposition, especially for the beginner. Another advantage is that as they are simple, so there is less to go wrong mechanically, and there are many survivors in reasonable condition. Most "cellarmans" date from the late 19th to early 20thC and were working tools more suited to the cellar than the dining room.

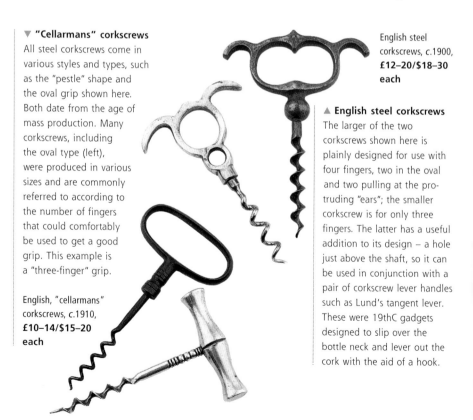

▼ "Cellarmans" corkscrews
All steel corkscrews come in various styles and types, such as the "pestle" shape and the oval grip shown here. Both date from the age of mass production. Many corkscrews, including the oval type (left), were produced in various sizes and are commonly referred to according to the number of fingers that could comfortably be used to get a good grip. This example is a "three-finger" grip.

English, "cellarmans" corkscrews, c.1910, **£10–14/$15–20 each**

English steel corkscrews, c.1900, **£12–20/$18–30 each**

▲ **English steel corkscrews**
The larger of the two corkscrews shown here is plainly designed for use with four fingers, two in the oval and two pulling at the protruding "ears"; the smaller corkscrew is for only three fingers. The latter has a useful addition to its design – a hole just above the shaft, so it can be used in conjunction with a pair of corkscrew lever handles such as Lund's tangent lever. These were 19thC gadgets designed to slip over the bottle neck and lever out the cork with the aid of a hook.

▼ Cast steel corkscrews

In 1905 the English firm of W. H. Plant produced the "Magic corkscrew" (which is so named on the hoop). It belongs to a category designed to remove the cork completely, extracting it by turning, not pulling. The design is interesting and it is a good example of how new types continued to be produced into the 20thC. The cast steel corkscrew (*right*) dating from 1880, is known as the "eyebrow" for reasons which should be obvious.

Left: cast steel "Magic" corkscrew, 1905 patent, **£70–90/$105–135**; right: cast steel corkscrew, *c.*1880, **£18–22/$28–32**

Polished steel folding corkscrew, *c.*1880, **£140–160/$210–240**

▲ Leather-cased folding corkscrew

This neat corkscrew is hinged and comes with its own leather case. A combination piece, it has a helical worm and also features a square railway carriage key and a wire or foil cutter. These fold out to form the handle for the corkscrew itself. It measures 5.75cm (2¼in) when closed and its case and excellent condition make it quite a prize.

▼ Bow corkscrews

The evidence of contemporary engravings tells us that the design of the bow corkscrew dates back to at least the 18thC. It would appear that most corkscrews made at that time were designed to be portable – the worm folds back inside the bow, which enables it to be carried safely in the pocket. The bow corkscrew was such a popular design that it continued to be made for a long time after its invention, though the shape of the bow itself may show considerable variation.

English, steel pocket folding bow corkscrews, *c.*1890, **£10–15/$15–22 each**

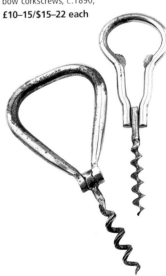

Corkscrews: waiters' friends

Even non-wine drinkers are likely to possess a corkscrew, even if it is only on a penknife. Here are some early examples of this ubiquitous tool. Not all of them, however, include a knife, but do incorporate some other useful tool. They can be considered the forerunners of the modern-day Swiss Army Knife. Also shown here is an example of one of the cork extraction methods that did not rely on the use of a worm. Some wine authorities and corkscrew experts are critical of these methods, which do not appear to be very successful when used today, and the fact that most modern corkscrews feature a traditional worm probably speaks for itself. However, modern corks are harder and denser than their older counterparts, so it is difficult to tell how successful they would have been in their day.

Brass-sided, pocket penknife and corkscrew, by I. Cutman, c.1890,
£35–45/ $55–70

◀ Pocket penknife and corkscrew

This combined penknife and corkscrew advertises the firm of A. & R. Thwaites & Co. Ltd. on one side, and has "Inventors of Soda Water" on the reverse. Such tools were made in large numbers for advertising purposes. Measuring 8cm (3½in) in length it also offers a small hooked blade ideal for cutting foil or wire from around the neck of a wine bottle.

▼ Folding knife and corkscrew

This French pocket knife combines a large blade, some 12cm (5in) in length, with a long spike and helical worm. The handle is shaped as a leg and has cow horn "scales", with brass "pinhead" decoration on one side. The top of the leg and the foot are in shaped brass. This example has great decorative appeal – the back steel "spine" is engraved with a leaf design and at the top of the spine is a little cast steel bumblebee. Such details add much to the desirability of this item.

French, folding cow horn-sided knife and corkscrew, stamped "Calmels a Laguiole", c.1880,
£170–190/ $255–285

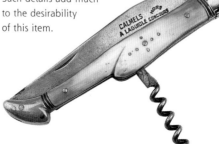

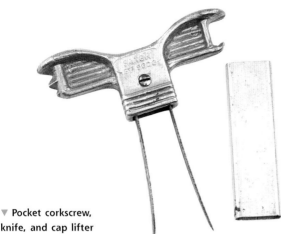

Cork extractors

- In earlier versions of the two-pronged cork extractor, both prongs are of the same length. In later versions, one may be slightly longer than the other.
- They are not easy to use, but those who have the knack swear by them.
- The French firm of Sanbri manufactured many of these types of cork extractors.

▼ Pocket corkscrew, knife, and cap lifter

This piece was made in the city of Sheffield, a major centre of steelmaking and of the cutlery industry in England. The production of such useful gadgets was a logical spin off for the cutlers' workshops. This combination piece was made for promotional purposes and has an advert for "No. 10 Scotch Whisky". It would probably have been given away with orders for the whisky from various establishments.

Pocket corkscrew, knife and cap lifter, by John Watts, c.1900, **£15–18/$22–28**

French, "Sanbri", tin-cased cork extractor, c.1920, **£18–24/$28–35**

▲ "Butler's Friend"

Not all methods of cork extraction rely on the use of a worm, and this is one example of an alternative method. The sprung metal prongs are inserted on either side of the cork, which lets in air and makes it easier to pull out the cork. A metal sheath guards the prongs when not in use. One useful aspect of these extractors is that they could also be used to re-insert the cork. For this reason, they are sometimes referred to as the "butler's friend", as it would be possible to remove the cork, sample some wine, top up the bottle and replace the cork without anyone noticing!

English, pocket folding corkscrew and cap lifter, by C.T. Willetts, 1921, **£60–80/$90–120**

▲ Pocket corkscrew and cap lifter

This gadget was made by Charles Thomas Willetts of Birmingham. It combines a corkscrew and crown cork remover with a cap lifter, and folds neatly for carrying in the pocket. The crown cork came into use c.1900, and removers soon became a feature of many of these combination pieces. When open, it acts as the handle to the corkscrew. It is nickel plated and stamped with its patent number (117694) and date between the hinges, allowing for easy identification.

"N⁰ 10" SCOTCH WHISKY

Corkscrews: Clough-type

The traditional way of manufacturing helical corkscrews essentially involved winding thick wire around a corkscrew to produce the desired result. In 1875, W. Rockwell Clough in the United States revolutionized corkscrew manufacture when he took out a patent on a new machine. Clough's machine could twist a piece of wire into a complete corkscrew in one simple operation. The impact of this invention on the industry was considerable on both sides of the Atlantic. Soon it was possible to mass-produce basic corkscrews at a much lower cost. Among the items shown here is a corkscrew with a codd bottle opener. This type of bottle was invented by Hiram Codd in 1870, and was designed for soft drinks. It featured a glass marble stopper kept in place by the pressure of gas, which had to be pushed down in order to release it.

American, turned wood and brass banded T-bar corkscrew, "Haff Patentee 1885", **£80–90/$120–135**

▲ **Haff corkscrew**
This is an example of the Edward P. Haff corkscrew. The patent was not strictly speaking on the corkscrew as a whole, but on the handle mount. Haff produced a diverse range in various styles and sizes. Although they are sometimes glued, this example is fastened with pins located on either side of a band. This method was the more common. It is named "Haff M'F'G Co. New York Patd apl. 14. 85 May 5th 85". It has a fine steel shaft with "bobbin" turning and a perfect helical worm.

▼ **Combination corkscrew and bottle opener**
This combination corkscrew and codd bottle opener features a codd bottle marble ejector at one end, which is hollow in order to allow the liquid to be poured through. Note the short pipe halfway down the nickel-plated shaft. The purpose of this is to release the sudden gush of carbonated air produced when the marble plunger is initially depressed into the bottle.

English, walnut-handled combination corkscrew and codd bottle marble depresser, patented by Matt Perking, c.1884, **£70–80/$105–120**

- Illustrated here are some Clough-type corkscrews with advertisements on the wooden sheaths.
- Some Clough-types bore advertisements around the bow, especially in the case of the smaller ones for use with medicine bottles, which were given away with the medicine.

▼ Clough corkscrew

This Clough corkscrew is made from a single piece of twisted wire and is complete with its original wooden sheath. The sheath features an advertisement for railway hotels, naming the "L.M.S. Hotels" company followed by a list of its establishments. Around the base of the sheath is "WRC Crown cork-opener Made in the USA pat. Mar 1 1910". The wire loop at the base of the sheath acts as the crown cork lifter. Crown corks, which comprised a cork and metal disc to seal the bottle, made their first appearance in 1900.

American, Clough, c.1910,
£25–30/$40–45

American, Walker's self-pulling bell cap, c.1900,
£20–30/$30–45

▲ Self-pulling corkscrew

This is a good example of the "self-pulling" corkscrew and the bell shape is a typical feature. This one was made by Edwin Walker and has a plain turned wooden handle with black lettering advertising "Babst of Milwaukee" on both sides. Instructions for use are given under the handle in an oval, reading "Don't pull, turn until cork is out". This bell cap was first patented in July 1893.

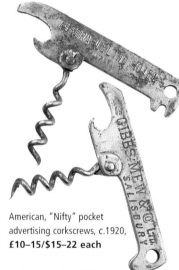

American, "Nifty" pocket advertising corkscrews, c.1920,
£10–15/$15–22 each

▲ Pocket advertising corkscrews

Clough's invention allowed the production of fairly sturdy and reliable corkscrews on a larger scale, and for lower cost than ever before. This in turn made the corkscrew an ideal medium for carrying advertising and as promotional gifts. These steel examples, made by Vaughan of Chicago, USA, were very easy to produce, and were made in a single stamping with a worm riveted to them.

Corkscrews: lever & concertina

Here are several examples of corkscrews that employed various mechanisms to assist the muscle power of the user. Some use levers, a principle that goes back to the time of Archimedes; the first example of the use of a lever to aid cork extraction dates from 1855 when Lund patented his "tangent lever". The concertina was another solution to the problem, and proved successful enough to spawn numerous versions in Britain, France and Germany. The collector should remember that the date of a patent is not necessarily the same as the date of manufacture: a successful design might have been made for many decades. Rival manufacturers also produced remarkably similar versions of successful designs, and could even copy them if the original patent had expired.

▼ Two-part lever corkscrew

This is one of several variations produced on the original tangent lever design by Lund. It is in two parts, namely the worm itself and a lever mechanism. The worm is screwed into the cork and is then withdrawn with the aid of the lever, which fits onto the bottle. A hook on the lever fits into a hole in the top of the worm.

English, Wolverson, brass and steel cork drawer, registered 1873,
£100–130/ $150–195

▲ "A. 1 Double Lever"

Many corkscrews incorporate levers to make the task of pulling the cork much easier. Some use a single lever, while others, such as on this example, use a double lever. The lever arms are raised by the action of screwing in the worm, and are lowered to draw the cork. This method proved to be very successful.

English, J. Heeley & Sons, copper finish, "A. 1 Double Lever", c.1890,
£100–120/ $150–180

▼ Weir's concertina corkscrew

During the late 19thC it became both feasible and affordable to produce corkscrews in various attractive finishes. These finishes, such as the copper version shown below, often show signs of wear over time. Nevertheless, this is an attractive example of the Weir concertina corkscrew, from a patent taken out by Marshall Weir in 1884 and manufactured by J. Heeley & Sons of Birmingham.

English, Marshall Weir, copper finish concertina by J. Heeley & Sons, c.1884,
£90–100/$135–150

French, nickel-plated, concertina "zigzag" corkscrew, c.1930,
£55–65/$85–100

▲ Concertina "zigzag" corkscrew

The concertina idea, invented in England, was taken up with enthusiasm in France where its popularity continued well into the 20thC, and new designs emerged. The "zigzag" was one of the more successful examples. The corkscrew shown here is in mint condition – an important factor. With its original box and instructions it would be even more valuable and worth perhaps twice as much.

- While they may have been effective, certain Weir-types were expensive to make, so were not always profitable for their makers.
- The "A. 1 Double Lever" was patented by J. Heeley & Sons of Birmingham in 1888 and is a valued addition to any collection.

▼ All-steel concertina corkscrew

This all-steel French concertina-type corkscrew is stamped "Ideal Brevete" on one bar. The handle is hinged and it has a bladed worm. This design was very popular and was produced in large numbers, so these corkscrews can be a very affordable way of adding a concertina-type to a collection.

French, all-steel concertina, c.1920,
£20–30/$30–45

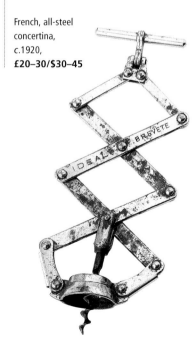

Corkscrews: brass figurals

These corkscrews would be a welcome addition to any collection. They all date from the 20thC, and many of them from the 1930s or later. Figurals were often produced as souvenirs of holidays or places of interest, but some are simply intended as interesting curiosities. They were inexpensive in their day, and mostly remain so today. Yet they should not be regarded solely as "cheap and cheerful" pieces, as they do reflect an important period of social change. They were produced at a time of rising living standards (war and depression notwithstanding), when people had the money to buy such items which, while they were often quite functional, were designed principally with ornament in mind. As well as being suitable for corkscrews, some of the figural designs were also used for bottle cap lifters (see pp56–57).

English 1930s cast brass figural corkscrews, ship and castle, **£12–20/ $18–30 each**

▶ **Souvenir corkscrews**
Here are two typical corkscrews of the type produced as souvenirs. Both examples feature the "eyebrow" grip (see p.39), and both have a hole or ring for hanging them on a wall. They are cast on one side only, the back being flat. Ships in particular were popular choices, and some can be found that depict specific famous vessels, such as HMS *Victory*, Nelson's flagship at the Battle of Trafalgar. The *Mayflower* ship was another very popular choice.

▼ **Animal figurals**
Animals have provided much inspiration to designers of figural corkscrews. Dogs and cats were popular products of the Birmingham factories where many of these English examples were made. The firm of Pearson-Page-Jewsbury was responsible for a good number of them. These stylized animals have typical design features of the Art Deco era.

English, dark bronzed animal figurals, cat and dachshund, c.1930, **£15–25/ $22–40 each**

Italian, aluminium clown two-arm lever corkscrew, c.1950, £120–140/$180–210

▲ **Clown lever corkscrew**
This exceptionally handsome and amusing barman's corkscrew is combined with a crown cap lifter, which is formed by the clown's mouth. The clown's bib has the words "cheers, salud, á votre santé, good luck, cin cin, gezondheid, skal, prosit" on it and the word "Hic!" is written on the back of the clown's head. This is a decorative example of the double lever type of corkscrew. The clown's arms rise as the worm is inserted, and when they are pushed down the cork is withdrawn.

▼ **"Key" corkscrew**
"Key" corkscrews are among the most interesting of figural pieces and, because of their appearance, it is possible for them to go unrecognized as corkscrews altogether. The key shank forms the sheath and unscrews to reveal the worm, and the shaped handle incorporates a cap lifter.

English, chrome-plated "key" corkscrew and bottle cap lifter, c.1950, £25–30/$40–45

American, Negbaur-type, c.1950, £25–30/$40–45

▲ **Gilded parrot corkscrew**
The design patent for this amusing type of corkscrew was issued originally to Manuel Avillar of New York in 1929, and was manufactured by Harry Negbaur. One of the parrot's eyes is an artificial ruby, while the other is a fake diamond. The parrot's bill forms a cap lifter and the corkscrew folds down behind its wings.

Corkscrews: multi-tools

Miniature corkscrews were being made as long ago as the 18thC and, in spite of their size, they were certainly intended to be functional rather than merely decorative. The 19thC saw the advent of the steam train and this, coupled with shorter working hours, meant that outings and picnics became popular. Corkscrew manufacturers responded to demands for small corkscrews that could be easily carried on a picnic and produced them in a variety of designs. The 18thC folding bow corkscrew (see below) retained its popularity and was joined by newer designs, including the Wright and Bailey roundlets, which contained a corkscrew and other useful tools within a neat cylindrical case.

▼ **Multi-tool folding bow corkscrew**
The folding bow corkscrew dates from the 18thC and this extremely useful 19thC example incorporates no fewer than eight tools. As well as a corkscrew, there is a hoof pick, buttonhook, screwdriver, auger, spike, gimlet, and leather hole punch. The whole item measures 7.5cm (3in) when closed. These multi-tool types might have as few as three tools, or as many as sixteen. Most corkscrews of the folding bow variety do not bear any marks, though a handful do.

English, faceted steel, multi-tool folding bow corkscrew, c.1830, **£350–380/ $525–570**

▼ **Miniature folding bows**
The small size of these pocket corkscrews suggests that they would have been used for opening medicine or perfume bottles. They were popular from the late 18thC onwards and were made in various shapes and sizes, some incorporating additional gadgets. The corkscrew below left has a buttonhook, a device that is not in widespread use today but was essential in the past. It was used for pulling buttons through button-holes for boots and gloves, a task that was more difficult then, given the stiff and heavy materials of the day.

Collection of English, miniature folding bow corkscrews, c.1830, **£100–120/ $150–180 each**

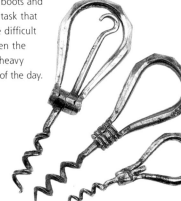

• Hollweg corkscrews
are quite an unusual
find, stamped examples
even more so, and
this will be reflected
in the high prices.
• Some of the tools in a
roundlet-type may be lost
over the years, which
will reduce the value.

Pressed silver-plated nickel
folding medicine spoon and corkscrew, c.1890, **£70–80/$105–120**

▼ Hollweg-type corkscrew

This type of corkscrew was
patented by Carl Hollweg
in the United States in 1891.
It was also patented in
England, but was produced
in Germany. The hinged
handle can be folded down
so that it surrounds the worm
and can be carried safely
in the pocket. Many bear
no marks, although some
examples are stamped
"Made Abroad" or "Germany".
They were made of steel
and measure approximately
9cm (3½in) in length.

German, pocket folding Hollweg-
type, marked "Patent Angemeldet
Made Abroad", c.1900,
£70–90/$105–135

▲ Folding medicine spoon
and corkscrew

While many corkscrews were
designed with medicines in
mind, this rare silver-plated
example seems particularly
fit for the purpose. The worm
folds neatly into the bowl of
the spoon, which has raised
lettering advertising various
drugs such as "Hazeline Cream,
Kepler Extract, Essence of
Malt, Cod Liver Oil...". It is
the same size as a teaspoon.
Spoons of this type were
often sold with medicines.

▼ Roundlets

The roundlet-type comprises
not only a corkscrew but also
various other tools, such as
a pair of tweezers, a spike, a
screwdriver or a gimlet. All of
these slot into one side of the
barrel and are stored inside
when not in use. Many of
them were made in metals
such as brass or steel, but
some were either of silver or
silver plate, and at least one
gold example is known.

Right: brass-cased pocket
roundlet and tools, c.1910,
£15–18/$22–28; left: engine-
turned, silver-cased roundlet,
maker Thomas Johnson, 1862,
£260–300/$390–450

Corkscrews: Continental

In the 20thC British factories produced vast numbers of corkscrews, while several famous designs were patented in the United States. However, some excellent and innovative corkscrews were also produced on the Continent, notably (and appropriately) in wine-producing countries. In France the best known manufacturer is J.H. Perille, and in Germany the most famous corkscrew is the "Monopol". Although the Monopoly works was in Steinbach-Hallenberg, most German corkscrew production is centred on Solingen, a large steel-producing area that is responsible for a number of interesting corkscrews, including the orange plastic example shown opposite. While many Continental firms were innovators, they also improved and developed existing ideas, and Continental corkscrews often provide affordable variations on popular designs.

German,
"Monopol",
c.1910,
**£15–25/
$22–40**

◀ **"Monopol"**
This corkscrew features a ring of ball bearings set into the top of the frame, which allows it to be turned more smoothly and makes it technically very efficient. These models also typically include a rubber insert where the bottom of the frame sits on the neck of the bottle, although this may long since have perished. The Usbeck family founded the Monopoly works in 1879 and produced both "Monopol" and "Hercules" corkscrews. "Monopols" dated from about 1880 onwards are quite common, and therefore affordable to collectors.

▶ **"Perille" triple propeller**
The "Perille" corkscrew is another quite common design, and therefore makes a good and inexpensive start to any collection. It was patented by J. Perille in 1876. Pictured here is an example of the open-frame type of corkscrew, which makes for easier cork removal. It is simple to operate, and the design allows the worm to be centred without difficulty. It has a distinctive shaped driving handle and three-winged lever collar tapped to the threaded shank for raising the cork.

French,
"Perille" triple propeller-type,
c.1920,
**£12–18/
$18–28**

French, steel, open frame "Hercules", c.1920, **£14–18/$20–28**

▲ **Spring-assisted "Hercules"**
This is an example of the spring-assisted corkscrews that were particularly popular with French and German manufacturers. As the worm is driven in, so the spring is compressed and this helps to draw the cork more easily. How much assistance a spring type really gave to the removal of the cork is a matter of debate. Many similarly-designed corkscrews are all steel, but this one has a turned wooden handle.

▼ **All-steel corkscrew**
This French corkscrew features a T-bar handle with a flip-over locking device in the centre. This locks the handle at the top of the threaded shaft when inserting the bladed worm into the cork. When the worm is fully inserted into the cork, the flange on the locking piece hits the top of the frame, thus enabling the threaded shaft to be drawn up through the handle, extracting the cork. It is stamped on the shoulder of the open frame on one side with the word "acier", which is French for "steel".

French, open frame corkscrew, c.1930, **£20–25/$30–40**

• Names can sometimes be misleading when dealing with Continental corkscrews. The name of "Columbus", for example, might be mistaken for an American make, but it is in fact German.
• Grandiose names were popular with makers; "Hercules" was a good one as it implied strength and was widely known.

German, corkscrew with plastic grip, c.1970, **£10–15/$15–22**

▲ **Sieger corkscrew**
This unusual corkscrew was made in Solingen, Germany. It has a bright orange coloured plastic grip and an inner spring sleeve, which unscrews from the handle grip to force the cork out of the bottle, once the cork has been fully penetrated by the worm. It has the moulded name "Sieger 600" on the top of the handle, and features the "Archimedean"-type worm (see p.61).

Corkscrews: Continental ~ 51

Corkscrews: straight pulls

Simply screw in the worm, pull, and enjoy your wine. The "straight pull" corkscrew is the simplest of all, so from a strictly technical point of view they are of less interest than the more elaborate corkscrews shown elsewhere. Yet they have been around since the 18thC and there is plenty of enjoyment to be had from the large number of styles and designs. There are seemingly endless combinations of shaft, worm and handle, the latter being available in an astonishing range of materials. This variety, coupled with the fact that they are generally not too expensive, makes straight pulls among the most collected of all corkscrews. Even though they are relatively unsophisticated, some straight pulls have included innovations that made them worthy of a patent – Samuel Henshall's being perhaps the most obvious example.

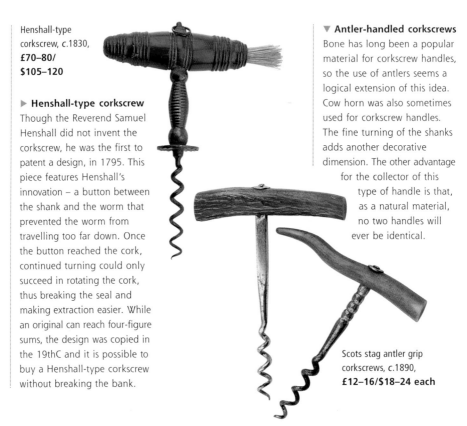

Henshall-type corkscrew, c.1830,
£70–80/
$105–120

▶ **Henshall-type corkscrew**
Though the Reverend Samuel Henshall did not invent the corkscrew, he was the first to patent a design, in 1795. This piece features Henshall's innovation – a button between the shank and the worm that prevented the worm from travelling too far down. Once the button reached the cork, continued turning could only succeed in rotating the cork, thus breaking the seal and making extraction easier. While an original can reach four-figure sums, the design was copied in the 19thC and it is possible to buy a Henshall-type corkscrew without breaking the bank.

▼ **Antler-handled corkscrews**
Bone has long been a popular material for corkscrew handles, so the use of antlers seems a logical extension of this idea. Cow horn was also sometimes used for corkscrew handles. The fine turning of the shanks adds another decorative dimension. The other advantage for the collector of this type of handle is that, as a natural material, no two handles will ever be identical.

Scots stag antler grip corkscrews, c.1890,
£12–16/$18–24 each

▼ Walnut-handled corkscrews

Straight pull corkscrews with wooden handles are readily available. Various kinds of wood were used for the handles, including lignum vitae, fruitwood, and walnut. While they lack the complexity of mechanical corkscrews, collectors should check the condition of the dusting brush and ensure that the handle is still secure; often a hole will be seen in one end of the handle, which indicates that the brush is missing.

English, turned walnut T-bar corkscrews, c.1880, **£25–30/$40–45 each**

English, barrel-turned fruitwood-handled corkscrews, c.1840, **£30–40/$45–60 each**

▲ Fruitwood-handled corkscrews

Wooden-handled corkscrews were often decorated by turning them on a lathe. Corkscrews of this type were made over a long period of time, and there is plenty of choice for the collector. They are much sought after, and seem to fit the popular notion of what an antique corkscrew should look like. For this reason they are frequently a first purchase, either as a gift or as the start of a collection.

▼ Vine root-handled corkscrew

The motif of grapes and vine leaves is common in wine-related antiques, but this corkscrew takes it a stage further by using a vine root as the handle. The gnarled root adds plenty of decorative appeal, and yet these cork-screws are quite inexpensive – possibly because they are still being produced today.

French vine root-handled corkscrew, "Siret. Rochforts/ Loire", c.1930, **£5–10/$8–15**

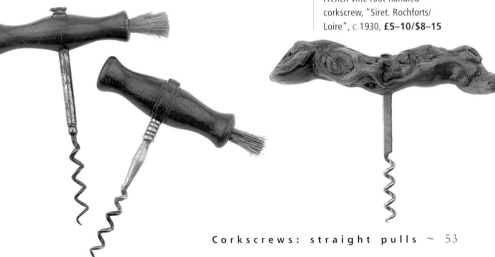

Corks & pourers

A cork that can be re-inserted into the bottle is the obvious solution for those that are not finished in one go – but there is no need for these to be plain. Decorative corks were produced in the 19thC, and surviving examples are desirable. But it was during the 20thC that drinks manufacturers came up with a really interesting array of corks designed to go with their products. Pourers were also produced, allowing the stoppered drink to be poured into a glass. A number of pourers were made as amusing novelties for the private household, but those designed for commercial use are more widely available. They were an ideal medium for advertising, keeping the name of the product in front of the drinker and bar staff at little cost. Sophistication and rarity are always important, so the more elaborate pourers and those advertising lesser-known products will always attract the most interest.

▼ **Silver-capped corks**
These corks would have been ideal for private, rather than commercial, use and are likely to appeal to collectors of small silver items as well as those interested in wine antiques in particular. They are hallmarked "London 1849", and bear a lion family crest. The corks are decorated quite delicately with a floral design and would certainly have been made for use in a gentleman's household. They are quite long, allowing for easier insertion and removal of the cork.

Silver-capped corks, 1849, **£160–180/ $240–270 pair**

▶ **Novelty cork and pourer**
Animals make ideal ornaments for novelty corks and pourers. The brass heraldic lion is Dutch, and makes an attractive and inexpensive start to a collection. The polar bear pourer is rather more valuable, not only because it is made of silver but it is also extremely rare and generally more elaborate. The drink is poured through the very delicately hinged bear's mouth, which opens and closes at the slightest tilt. It also incorporates a corkscrew.

Left: brass lion cork, c.1920, **£15–18/ $22–28;** right: silver polar bear pourer, c.1890, **£220–250/ $330–375**

There are few collectors of solely corks and pourers, but these items do find a place in many a general collection. The more elaborate they are the better, and condition is extremely important, especially in the case of the more commonplace items. Amusing Swiss and Italian carved pine figural cork stoppers are also collected, especially if they are articulated.

Right: Beefeater gin pourer, c.1960, £20–25/$30–40; left: Dickens character pourer, c.1930, £15–20/$22–30

▲ China pourers

The Staffordshire potteries produced china pourers such as these. The Wade factory, in particular, produced many of these items, which were made in large numbers and were inexpensive to manufacture. The "Beefeater" was designed for commercial use, being the name of a famous brand of gin – the spirit pours out of a hole in his hat. The Charles Dickens character is "Bob Cratchit", from A Christmas Carol; the drink comes through his nose, which has a single, large nostril for the purpose.

▼ Whisky pourer

This china piece is in the form of a grouse, and is a commercial pourer designed and made by the Wade factory for the makers of "Famous Grouse" scotch whisky. The drink is poured through a hole in the rock on which the grouse sits. Wade became known for the manufacture of small ceramic collectables, including animal figures, and was therefore well-suited to this kind of production. In common with many firms, "Famous Grouse" produced a range of pieces, such as water jugs and other accessories, and still offers items, including pourers, today.

Whisky pourer, c.1970, £20–25/$30–40

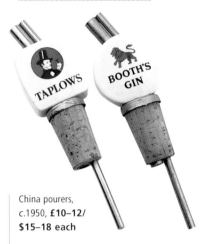

China pourers, c.1950, £10–12/$15–18 each

▲ 20thC china pourers

These pourers were for named brands and would have been used commercially. In the case of the "White Horse", the drink is poured "straight from the horse's mouth". The "Taplows" pourer features the company logo, and with this and the "Booth's Gin" example, the drink pours from the metal tube running through the stopper.

Bottle cap lifters

The crown cap was invented in 1900, and many firms went into production with suitable openers. Several of the multi-tool gadgets described on pages 48 and 49 include openers for this purpose, but here we see a selection of cap lifters that were specifically designed with crown caps. A great many of these items were intended for advertising and other promotional purposes, and were given away as freebies. Some advertise drinks' firms that no longer exist, and are therefore of historic interest; other cap lifters feature the names of well-known brands such as "Coca-Cola", which are of interest to the many collectors who specialize in memorabilia related to famous beverages. Being small and cheap to produce, these bottle openers soon attracted the attention of the souvenir industry. Vast numbers were produced as inexpensive yet useful reminders of tourist attractions and holiday resorts.

Left: "Blackpool" cap lifter, c.1948, **£10–14/$15–20**; right: Scotsman, c.1930, **£12–15/$18–22**

▶ **Souvenir cap lifters**
In the years following the Second World War, people in Britain could once again begin to enjoy the luxury of holidays by the sea, and Blackpool was perhaps the most popular destination of them all. This cap lifter depicts Blackpool Tower, the town's best known landmark. The Scotsman in traditional Highland dress is painted brass-plated cast iron. As a fairly generic piece, he would have been suitable for any Scottish tourist attraction.

▼ **Brass cap lifters**
These openers both date from the 1930s which, economic difficulties notwithstanding, was an era when trains and buses took increasing numbers of working people on outings and holidays. Here are two examples from the burgeoning souvenir industry that supplied a considerable demand. Both are cast in brass, while the example bearing a Welsh coat of arms is also enamelled.

Right: Welsh coat of arms, c.1935; left: Isle of Jersey, c.1930, **£12–14/ $18–20 each**

▼ French bottle openers

The bottle opener on the left has a heraldic theme, and is double-sided in cast brass, inset with black leather. The shape suggests that it would have been useful as a corkscrew, and indeed a matching corkscrew was also made. It is a sizeable piece, being nearly 15cm (6in) in length. The nickel opener (right) is in the form of a cockerel, France's national emblem. Intricate relief work picks out the detail and texture in the plumage.

Left: large heraldic opener, c.1920, **£16–20/$24–30**; right: French cockerel opener, c.1960, **£16-£18/$24–28**

Right: Greek, bronze owl, c.1960, **£10–14/$15–20**; left: horse's head, c.1930, **£12–15/$18–22**

▲ Animal openers

Although the Greek opener shown here is relatively modern, the decorative appeal of this cloisonné piece (coloured enamel inside a wire surround) makes it roughly equivalent in value to the older horse's head model. An owl has a beautiful red lustre in its wing plumage and, as the ancient symbol of Athens, was the inspiration for this piece. Horse's heads were popular with designers; this double-sided cap lifter shows a horse with a "Trojan-style" mane.

▼ Deco-style nude female and boy cap lifters

The opener showing a nude female figure is cast brass and double-sided. Its most unusual feature is that it was designed to stand upright on a table and it has a square integral base for this purpose. The boy in a top hat is made of turned wood and he has moveable arms. Numerous variations on the theme were produced, and other popular characters included a guardsman.

Right: nude female, c.1930, **£17–19/$25–29**; left: boy in top hat, c.1950, **£15–17/$22–25**

Other items for the collection

For the collector there are many objects and artefacts that do not fit into any particular category, but which nevertheless deserve a place in the collection. Lovers of wine-related antiques will collect almost anything to do with the subject. Even old wine merchants' ledgers are of interest. The wine trade has inspired many an artist, and pictures of various kinds are certainly appealing, including silhouettes, old prints, and engravings. As well as dealers in wine-related antiques, architectural antiques specialists are worth considering for carvings and other objects that might have been removed from a demolished bar or an old wine merchant's premises. From pictures and porcelain to carvings and silver, the collecting of wine-related antiques is a multi-disciplinary activity. The common thread is the theme, and as long as it is relevant to that theme, anything is fair game.

▼ **Pottery sherry barrel**
This crimson Staffordshire pottery sherry barrel provided an appealing way to serve this drink. It was made for commercial use and would have seen used in a bar. Any items which were used in the trade are of interest to the collector, including all kinds of bar paraphernalia. This barrel would still be quite useable for its original purpose and has more than just ornamental value. As with any ceramics, chips and cracks will devalue such pieces, though minor damage may be acceptable. Many have been converted into table lamps.

Sherry barrel,
c.1870,
£270–275/
$405–415

▶ **19thC silhouette**
Silhouette art first appeared in the 18thC, and the name derives from that of the miserly French Finance Minister, Etienne de Silhouette. August Edouart (1789–1861) is regarded as the greatest silhouette artist of all, but the art form gained popularity and was widely practised. The silhouette grew out of science as well as art, as it relates to the study of physiognomy and the notion that a person's profile could reflect the character of the individual. This portly gentleman, seen enjoying his glass of wine, has great charm.

Silhouette in a maple frame,
c.1840,
£275–300/
$415–450

Head of Bacchus, c.1750,
£850–£900/$1,275–1,350

▲ **Head of Bacchus**
Bacchus, as the god of wine,
is a figure who can be
expected to provide inspiration
for wine-related collectables.
This magnificent carved
wooden head, dating from
the mid 18thC, may well have
graced the premises of a wine
merchant. It is beautifully
carved and would add a nice
decorative touch to the home
of any wine enthusiast. Such
pieces are often popular with
interior designers working on
commercial premises such as
bars and restaurants.

▼ **Porcelain figure**
In spite of his 18thC costume,
this porcelain figure of a wine
merchant dates from the late
19thC. He is shown uncorking
a bottle of wine, with a basket
by his side. The piece bears
the mark that is generally
associated with the Meissen
factory. Coloured versions of
this figure are known, and are
comparatively common. This
rarer plain white figure is one
of a pair, its companion being
a figure of a dairymaid.

Porcelain figure, c.1880,
£750–800/$1,125–1,200

Silver-plated cocktail shaker,
c.1920, **£120–140/$180–210**

▲ **Art Deco cocktail shaker**
The 1920s was the decade
that spawned the Art Deco
style and the rise in popularity
of the cocktail. Cocktail shakers
are collectable in their own
right, and the 1920s and '30s
saw the production of shakers
in many unusual and
imaginative forms, such as
a penguin or a lighthouse.
This model is English and
is in a useable condition;
it features an ice strainer.

Where to buy & see

MUSEUMS

Harveys Wine Museum
Harvey House
12 Denmark St
Bristol BS1 5DQ UK
tel: 0117 9275036
www.soc.surrey.ac.uk/
~scs1sp/HWM

Musée du Tire-Bouchon
Domaine de la Citadelle
84560 Ménerbes, France
tel: (0033) 490 724158

Museum of Art and Design
Korkeavuorenkatu 23
00130 Helsinki, Finland
tel: (00358) 9 622 05 425
www.designmuseum.fi
(19thC British corkscrews)

Napa Valley Museum
55 Presidents Circle
Yountville, CA 94559 USA
tel: (001) 707 944 0500
www.napavalleymuseum.org

**Napa County Historical
Society Museum**
1219 First St
Napa, CA 94559 USA
tel: (001) 707 224 1739

Sharpsteen Museum
1311 Washington St
Calistoga
CA 94515 USA
tel: (001) 707 942 5911
www.sharpsteen-museum.org

Victoria and Albert Museum
Cromwell Road
South Kensington
London SW7 2RL UK
tel: 020 7942 2000
www.vam.ac.uk

Wine Museum Osaka
Fureai Minato-Kan 1–10–12
Nanko-kita Suminoe-ku
Osaka, Japan
tel: (0081) 6613 2411

COLLECTORS' CLUBS

**Canadian Corkscrew
Collectors Club**
2757 West 2nd Ave
Vancouver
British Columbia, Canada
www.bullworks.net/virtual/cccc

Helix Scandinavia
Kaponjärgatan 4 F
S–413 02 Göteborg Sweden
tel: (0046) 0 3113 3490

DEALERS

Christopher Sykes Antiques
The Old Parsonage, Woburn
Milton Keynes MK17 9QL UK
tel: 01525 290259/290467
www.sykes-corkscrews.co.uk
(Specialists in corkscrews
and wine-related antiques)

Antiques and Art Australia
885–9 High St
Armadale 3143
Victoria Australia

tel: (0061) 3 9500 0522
www.antique-art.com.au

INTERNET RESOURCES

Virtual Corkscrew Museum
www.corkscrew@bullworks.net

Bacchus Antiques
www.corkscrews@bacchus-
antiques.com

**Don Bull's Virtual
Corkscrew Museum**
www.bullworks.net/virtual.htm

Joe Paradi's Corkscrewnet
www.corkscrewnet.com

Patricia Harbottle
www.corkscrews.uk.co

The Corkscrew Centre
www.corkscrewcentre.com

www.corkscrew.com

Ebay www.ebay.com

AUCTION HOUSES

Christie's South Kensington
85 Old Brompton Road
London SW7 3LD UK
tel: 020 7581 7611
www.christies.com

Christie's East
219 East 67th St
New York, NY 10021 USA
tel: (001) 212 606 0400

What to read

Here is a selection of books on wine-related antiques. Some of them are suitable for those new to the subject, others are more specialist and will be invaluable as your interest develops.

Berston, B. & Ekman, P.
Scandinavian Corkscrews
(Tryckenforlaget, 1994)

Bull, D. The Ultimate
Corkscrew Book (Schiffer, 1999)

Butler, R. & Walkling, G.
The Book of Wine Antiques
(Antique Collectors' Club,
Woodbridge, Suffolk, 1986,
reprinted 1993)

Coldicott, P.
A Guide to Corkscrew Collecting
(Stockbridge, Hants, 1993)

De Sanctis, P. & Fantoni, M.
The Corkscrew: A Thing of Beauty
(Marzorati Editore, 1990)

Dumbrell, R.
Understanding Antique
Wine Bottles
(Antique Collectors' Club,
Woodbridge, Suffolk, 1983)

Guilian, B.
Corkscrews of the Eighteenth
Century: Artistry in Iron and Steel
(Whitespace Publishing, 1995)

Johnson, H.
The World Atlas of Wine
(Mitchell Beazley, 1971)

O'Leary, F.
Corkscrews (Schiffer, 1996)

Olive, G.
French Corkscrew Patents
1828–1974
(First Edition, 1995)

Perry, E.
Corkscrews and Bottle Openers
(Shire, 1980, reprinted 2000,
Princes Risborough, Bucks)

Peters, F.
German Corkscrew Patents/German
Corkscrew Registrations (Beheermy
Pintex Publishing, 1997)

Penzer, N. M.
The Book of the Wine Label
(Home & Van Thal., 1947)

Pinto, E. H.
Treen & Other Wooden Bygones,
(Bell & Hyman, 1969)

Pumpenmeier, K.
Deutscher Gebraumusterschutz
fur Korkenzieher 1891–1945
(Erschienen im
Selbstverlag, 1997)

Wallis, F.
British Corkscrew Patents
from 1795
(Vernier Press, 1997)

Watney, B. & Babbidge, H.
Corkscrews for Collectors
(Sotheby's, London, 1993)

Glossary

Archimedean worm A bladed spiral thread on a central core
Bell The cap on the shaft of American self-pulling corkscrews, so called because of its shape
Bladed worm A corkscrew thread that is broad, forming an edge

Bow A rounded metal handle on a simple corkscrew, commonly seen on the pocket folding variety, when it is also sometimes known as a harp
Brevet French abbreviation of "brevet d'invention", or patent
Bronzed A lacquer finish on steel
Brush Set in one end of a corkscrew handle, and usually

of hog bristle, the brush was used to clear away debris from around the neck of a bottle and for dusting off labels
Button Associated with "Henshall"-type corkscrews, this is a circular plate set just above the worm. It aids extraction of the cork by compressing and turning it in the bottle

Centre worm Formed by lathe-turning a bladed worm from a column of steel

Champagne tap or screw Device for obtaining small amounts of champagne from a bottle without opening it. It has a tap at one end and a point at the other, which can be pushed or screwed through the cork

Compound lever Concertina mechanisms or lazy tongs

Double action A type of corkscrew that both pierces and extracts a cork in one action by turning the handle in one direction only

Double lever A corkscrew which has two lever arms

D.R. Found on German corkscrews, this is an abbreviation for Deutsches Reich, or German Empire. See also "G.M." which is often also included

Eyebrow handle Corkscrew with curved handle, shaped rather like a pair of raised eyebrows

Female-threaded handle In which the shaft screws up through the handle to extract the cork

Figurals A term which is applied to certain corkscrews with decorative handles

Fluted worm A worm with grooves

Frame A frame surrounds the worm in certain types of corkscrews. Some are "open" while others form a barrel. The lower end rests on the

neck of the bottle as the cork is pulled. The top of a frame is referred to as the oulder

G.M. Found on German corkscrews, this abbreviation stands for "Gebrauchsmuster", or registered design; utility model (see also D.R.)

Gesetzlich Geschutz Patent registered

Hélice déposé Patented helix or screw

Helical worm A spiral with a rounded section and no sharp edges, unlike a bladed worm

Hermaphrodite screw Used in double action corkscrews, this has both male and female threads: female to the thread on the shaft of the cork worm and male to the outer frame

Left-hand screw A screw that turns in an anti-clockwise direction

Lever corkscrew Any corkscrew which employs a lever to assist cork removal. It could be a single lever, or a double lever with two side arms. Or, it could be a two-piece lever which features long, pivoted handles which are brought together to provide leverage to the corkscrew itself

Lignum vitae Hard, dense tropical wood, once thought to have life-giving properties, hence the name

Miniatures Corkscrews commonly used for medicines, perfumes or ink bottles, or as trinkets

Modéle déposé Patent or trade mark protection

M.M. Dép. or M. & M. Dép Marque et modéle déposés

Pat. Ang. Patent Angemeldet (Patent Pending)

Peg and worm A type of portable corkscrew. The peg is inserted into the worm when not in use, and can be inserted into a hole at the top of the worm to form a handle when required

Rack and pinion Mechanism for converting circular into rectilinear motion (or vice-versa)

Roundlet A small barrel corkscrew

Self-puller Type of corkscrew, especially popular in the United States, with a bell cap on the shaft, designed to enable corks to be removed by twisting, rather than pulling

Solid cut A worm that has been turned on a lathe from a piece of steel

Speed worm Screw with a steep pitch, designed for speed of use, and commonly seen on bar corkscrews

Spike Often found on combination pieces for breaking wires, string, sealing wax, etc

Worm Also known as the screw, is the metal part that penetrates the cork. It is made in a spiral or helix shape, and is used in one form or another in most corkscrews

Index

Acknowledgments

All pictures photographed by Steve Tanner (assisted by Lucille) for Octopus Publishing Group Ltd,
using articles in the stock of Christopher Sykes Antiques, Woburn, Bedfordshire.